REFLECTIONS ON THE HOLY SPIRIT

REFLECTIONS
ON THE
HOLY SPIRIT

Meditations on the Fruit of the Holy Spirit
Deacon Steve Greco
With Katie Hughes

DEDICATION

This book is dedicated to all the people involved in Spirit Filled Hearts Ministry who have influenced my love for Jesus.

I want to especially thank my wife Mary Anne who is always the foundation of my life.

I also am extremely thankful for our friend Katie Hughes who is filled with the Holy Spirit. Without her help, this book never would have been completed.

CONTENTS

ACKNOWLEDGMENTS

I want to thank Katie Hughes for her tremendous contributions with this book and for the editing of Michael Aimola and Cindy Brauer.

FOREWARD
By Katie Hughes

Deacon Steve Greco has the joy of the Lord in every step he takes, and he isn't one to be shy when it comes to evangelizing friends, family or perfect strangers. He has spent his adult life sharing the "Good News of Jesus Christ" with nearly everyone he encounters. Whether he is praying with individuals, speaking to large or small groups of people or leading prayer meetings at his local parish, he is nothing but passionate for sharing the Word of God. His love for God's people and wanting to touch the hearts of all those he encounters has not gone unnoticed. Some of his best examples of evangelization are on airplanes, restaurants and supermarkets. Deacon Steve's hope is that a fire will ignite the hearts of all those who read this book.

Reflections on the Holy Spirit can be the catalyst for the spiritually hungry. This book will help you on your journey to experience the power of the Holy Spirit. As you begin to read this book, pray to the Holy Spirit. Open your heart and ask the Holy Spirit to share His wisdom. Allow the Living

Word to speak to you and abide in your heart, soul and mind.

Deacon Steve Greco has spent his adult life following the footsteps of Jesus by the power of the Holy Spirit! If you have had the pleasure of listening to Deacon Steve Greco in person, on the radio, his audio CDs or reading his first book "365 Days of Praise," you would have heard Deacon Steve say "translated from the Greek into English the word 'power' means DYNAMITE!" How exciting to know that the Holy Spirit is powerful and explosive. As you read this book, allow the fire and the love of God to empower your life.

Scripture is meant to dwell in you, because it is the true living Word. Jesus lived among us and changed hearts with His words, actions and His love. Think of Jesus leading you to His Father in heaven each moment you breathe. Allow the power of the Holy Spirit to enlighten your soul as you read each verse of Holy Scripture

To live in the "Spirit" may be an unfamiliar phrase. To live in the Spirit is to abide in the Lord. The fruit of living in the Spirit is to live in God's love, joy peace, patience, kindness, generosity, faithfulness, gentleness, self-control. Followers of

Christ are not perfect but can strive for this perfection that Jesus demonstrated.

Deacon Steve demonstrates, the power of God's Holy Spirit in the scriptures. He prayerfully asks for each scripture to be revealed to you as an individual reader. His prayer is that when you read the scriptures and reflection, a special message of love, hope and encouragement is given to you. The purpose of this book is to know that you are loved by God and that the words in the holy scriptures of God are for you.

Deacon Steve, through the power of the Holy Spirit, shows us the benefits of living in the Spirit. He helps us take a closer look at the life we can live in the Spirit by examining scriptures that focus on the fruit of the Holy Spirit. Allow the transformation of your life to unfold as you bear the fruit of the Spirit.

INTRODUCTION

> In contrast, the fruit of the Spirit is love, joy, peace, patience, kindness, generosity, faithfulness, gentleness, self-control. Against such there is no law.
> *Galatians 5:22-23*

As we meditate on this passage from Galatians, we realize there is so much more we need to understand regarding each fruit of the Holy Spirit. For example, what does it mean to receive the fruit of love, joy or peace?

This book was written to assist the reader in examining Scripture that relates to each fruit of the Holy Spirit and how it applies to our lives. We recommend reading one page each day as a meditation, focusing on the desire of the Holy Spirit to transform us into the image and love of our Savior Jesus Christ.

LOVE

When we think about love, we think of emotion. Love is intense. Fervent. Passionate. When we think of Christian love we think in terms of unconditional or "agape" love—a reality not based upon prerequisites or circumstances. Unconditional love is the love Christ has for us. It is not a season or an emotion that comes and goes. It is a reality that lasts forever.

As you read these pages, meditate on how much you are loved by God and how much you love Him. Focus on how you take the love of God and apply it to your love of others. Learn what it means to love God with all your heart, mind, soul and strength and how to love your neighbor as yourself.

Love

1 Corinthians 13:8 "Love never fails...."

When we love with the Lord's love we are always successful. Jesus knows our heart and how we desire to love him and his people passionately. It is important to ask Jesus to show us how to love through his Sacred Heart.

Lord, may your Holy Spirit guide us as we reflect upon your message of unfailing love. We ask that you transform us to be a powerful conduit of your love.

_____

_____

_____

_____

_____

_____

_____

Psalm 91:7 "Though a thousand fall at your side, ten thousand at your right hand, near you it shall not come."

God loves us so much that we are protected by God no matter how many enemies we have. We are His children, protected by His love!

Lord, open our heart to a better understanding of Your everlasting love. May the Holy Spirit show us how You protect us throughout our lives. May we recognize Your powerful love through the most difficult times. Jesus, we know You are near.

_____

_____

_____

_____

_____

_____

1 Corinthians 13:7 "It bears all things, believes all things, hopes all things, endures all things."

A significant part of life is overcoming challenges and pain. With the love of Christ at the center of our lives and relationships, we have the strength to endure in the "joy of the Lord."

Lord, may Your merciful love shower us with Your grace. Through Your love, we know that all things are possible. Holy Spirit, reveal the great power of God's love to us so we can truly be faith-filled disciples.

_____

_____

_____

_____

1 Corinthians 13:4".....It is not jealous, [love] is not pompous, it is not inflated."

To truly love means that we put the object of our love's interests first, without hesitation! Love is selfless and always putting the other person first. Do you love with a pure heart? Are you single-minded with devoting your life to putting people first?

Lord, You are our Creator and you created all things out of love and mercy. Help us to love freely with your love. Holy Spirit, show us the way to have agape love for all your people so they will know how much you love them.

_____

_____

_____

Psalm 91:12 "With their hands they shall support you, lest you strike your foot against a stone."

We are loved by the Lord so much that He puts a shield around us. Do not fear. God is protecting you at all times.

Lord, we ask that you guide us to an understanding of the incredible love You have for us. Help us trust you with all of our struggles and relationships to allow your will to take over our lives.

_____

_____

_____

_____

_____

_____

_____

_____

1 Corinthians 16:14 "Your every act should be done with love."

Love is the foundation of all that we say and do when we follow the Lord! Each moment of each day we must strive to be in the presence of God. When we are in his presence, his love flows through us!

Lord, may we be in your presence in everything we do and may we be the channel of your love always.

_____

_____

_____

_____

_____

_____

_____

_____

LOVE

Colossians 3:14 "And over all these put on love, that is the bond of perfection."

God is love. It is important we ask God to fill us with his love. We can be assured, that when we ask for his love, we will receive it. When we let God fill us with His love, we follow His will in all that we do.

Lord, help us put on the gift of love in everything we think, say and do. We desire to embody your love for all people.

_____

_____

_____

_____

_____

_____

_____

1 John 4:16 "...God is love, and whoever remains in love remains in God and God in him."

To receive what God has promised us, it is mandatory that we say yes to the unwavering and unconditional love he has for us.   Once we say yes, we must remember that it is a daily necessity to be open to the love of God.

Teach us Lord to say yes to your love daily. Fill us with your Holy Spirit so that your love abides   in us for eternity.

_____

_____

_____

_____

_____

_____

1 John 4:18 "There is no fear in love, but perfect love drives out fear because fear has to do with punishment, so one who fears is not yet perfect in love."

Ask Jesus to take away your fear and fill you with his love. Our Lord drives out all fear in us and replaces it with his intense and eternal love.

We praise you God for being the God of love and for healing us of our fears.

_____

_____

_____

_____

_____

_____

_____

_____

1 John 3:18 "Children, let us love not in word or speech but in deed and truth."

It is not what we say but what we do. Do we love intensely, and do we demonstrate that love to everyone we encounter? This is both our mission and purpose in life. We must love God, with all our heart, soul, might, and strength. This allows us to love our neighbors as ourselves.

Help us Lord to always show your love in all our actions and what we do daily.

_____

_____

_____

_____

_____

_____

_____

LOVE

1 John 5:3 "For the love of God is this, that we keep his commandments. And his commandments are not burdensome."

We must understand that God's commandments are meant to help us love Him without sin. It is important to ask God for his grace, in order to follow his commandments daily.

Lord, help us to follow your commandments so that we are living in your righteousness.

_____

_____

_____

_____

_____

_____

_____

Ephesians 4:2 "With all humility and gentleness, with patience, bearing with one another through love."

God is always gentle and loving to us and teaches us to do the same with all His people.   It is essential to ask the Holy Spirit for the grace required to do God's will. We can be assured that we will receive the fruit of the Spirit; Love.

Help us God and empower us with your love and patience so that we depict your love in all our actions.

_____

_____

_____

_____

_____

_____

_____

LOVE

1 Peter 4:8 "Above all, let your love for one another be intense, because love covers a multitude of sins.

When we love God and His people intensely, we are covered and filled with the love of God.

Though we are sinners, we can still be used by God to love his people. God is merciful and will bless you when you say yes to loving fervently.

Teach us Lord how to love intensely, so that we may be in Your will daily.

_____

_____

_____

_____

_____

Ephesians 3:17 "and that Christ may dwell in your hearts through faith; that you, rooted and grounded in love."

Love is our foundation. It is the way, the truth and the life. We must be rooted in love. Think about having your actions each day rooted in the love of Jesus.

We praise you Lord for your unconditional love in us and for giving us the gift of love through faith.

_____

_____

_____

_____

_____

_____

_____

_____

Romans 12:9 "Let love be sincere: hate what is evil, hold on to what is good."

You cannot "fake" love. Seek it with all your heart and soul and avoid all evil in your lives. The Holy Spirit leads us to holiness and Jesus. Strive for holiness with our thoughts, words, and actions.

Help us Lord in our desire to love with your love and avoid evil in our life.

_____

_____

_____

_____

_____

_____

_____

_____

1 Corinthians 13:2 "And if I have the gift of prophecy and comprehend all mysteries and all knowledge, if I have faith so as to move mountains but do not have love, I am nothing."

We can have every gift in the world, be rich beyond belief and have every spiritual gift, but without love, we have nothing of true importance.

Thank You Lord for teaching us that without love we have nothing. Help us to seek love as our top priority.

_____

_____

_____

_____

_____

_____

John 15:12 "This is my commandment: love one another as I love you."

God is the source of all love. Jesus came to us to show us how to love his people. As we receive the love of the Lord, we are to take that love and love intensely God and one another.

Open our heart Lord, so that we may love others with your unconditional, fervent love.

_____

_____

_____

_____

_____

_____

_____

2 Thessalonians 3:5 "May the Lord direct your hearts to the love of God and to the endurance of Christ."

To love fervently, we must surrender our heart to the Sacred Heart of Jesus and His intense, enduring love. Ask Jesus to increase his love in your heart. Let him lead you.

Lord, we seek your Sacred Heart with all of our heart so that we may love you and others with your love.

_____

_____

_____

_____

_____

_____

_____

Isaiah 43:4a "Because you are precious in
my eyes and honored, and I love you,
I give people in return for you
and nations in exchange for your life."

Our human understanding cannot
comprehend how much God loves us.
When we are filled with his love we
recognize the joy it brings us. Rejoice and
be glad!

Help us, Lord, to meditate on how much
You love us so that we may feel your
infinite love at all times.

_____

_____

_____

_____

_____

_____

Romans 8:38-39 "For I am convinced that neither death, nor life, nor angels, nor principalities, nor present things, nor future things, nor powers, nor height, nor depth, nor any other creature will be able to separate us from the love of Christ Jesus our Lord."

God's love is total and complete, all-encompassing and comprehensive. It is important to learn how to praise God forever for His love of us!

We do not deserve your great love for us. Help us love your people with your love each day of our life!

_____

_____

_____

_____

My wife Mary Anne got a message from the Lord that the word "joy" means "Jesus Over You." What does that mean? How does it relate to the Christian walk? What is the difference between joy and happiness? Joy, indeed, is associated with God's abundant grace. When we have joy, we experience Jesus within us, showering us with His love, filling us with His grace and light. Our hearts feel like bursting.

Joy is not dependent upon circumstances, while happiness is based upon events and does not last. Joy lasts forever. It can never be taken away from us. When we surrender our heart and soul to Jesus, we are filled with Him and He gives us His joy. We desire to praise and worship Him, like angels on high, announcing His "Good News" for all to hear.

John 15:11 "I have told you this so that my joy may be in you and your joy may be complete."

The joy of the Lord gives us the strength to endure anything life presents to us. Let Jesus restore you and be filled with his Holy Spirit. Rejoice!

Lord, may we receive your joy so we can truly abide in you. We surrender our hearts to You and lift up our worries as a sacrifice. We trust in your plan and know that you are our everlasting joy.

_____

_____

_____

_____

_____

_____

_____

Nehemiah 8:10 "Do not be saddened this day, for rejoicing in the LORD is your strength."

Know this, Jesus is your future. All circumstances will pass away, but Jesus gives you everlasting joy. When we let the joy of the Lord fill our heart, we are filled with the Holy Spirit.

Holy Spirit, we pray for the grace to receive your joy every day. May we not be distracted by sadness, but know you are with us, waiting for us to turn to you, so you can show us how to live a joyful life.

_____

_____

_____

_____

_____

Philippians 4:4 "Rejoice in the Lord always, I shall say it again: rejoice!"

No matter what is happening to us, when we rejoice in the Lord, we are praising, trusting and loving Him! We are saying, "I believe!"

Lord, help us to trust in your righteousness so we can rejoice and believe in the joy you have for us. May we realize that you conquer all evil; we need not fear!

_____

_____

_____

_____

_____

_____

_____

_____

1 Thessalonians 5:18 "In all circumstances give thanks, for this is the will of God for you in Christ Jesus."

Rejoicing through all circumstances is possible when you call on the Lord to increase your faith. When we give thanks, we rejoice in what God is doing in each circumstance of our lives.

Lord, teach us to be thankful for the challenges in our life. Though we may not understand your ways, lead us to a life of trust in you, and may we rejoice knowing "Thy will be done."

_____

_____

_____

_____

_____

James 1:2"Consider it all joy, my brothers, when you encounter various trials."

When we experience trials, we learn to persevere and to rely on the Lord, which leads to joy in him!

Holy Spirit, show us the wisdom to know that the trials in our lives bring us ultimate joy and endurance. Teach us to rejoice that all things are possible with you by our side.

_____

_____

_____

_____

_____

_____

_____

Romans 15:13 "May the God of hope fill you with all joy and peace in believing so that you may abound in hope by the power of the Holy Spirit."

When we trust in the Lord, we have hope, which leads to peace and joy by the power of His love and Holy Spirit.

Our Lord and our God, show us the way to hope in you. Remove the distractions in our lives that lead us away from your joy.

_____

_____

_____

_____

_____

_____

_____

Proverbs 10:28 "The hope of the just brings joy."

We are living out our baptism as holy and just people. When we hope, we do not fear. When we hope, we are filled with love and joy!

In times of distress remind us of the power you have in our lives. Holy Spirit, guide us toward the heart of Jesus. Help us surrender our life to your love and rejoice in you, so that we may obtain the hope of the just.

_____

_____

_____

_____

_____

_____

Psalm 27:6b "I will offer in his tent, sacrifices with shouts of joy."

When we sacrifice our will for the will of the Lord, we will shout for joy for all eternity! When we die to ourselves it is the beginning of all joy.

Holy Spirit, give us the courage and strength to surrender each moment of every day for your glory. Help us to realize you are our everything.

_____

_____

_____

_____

_____

_____

_____

_____

Philemon 1:7 "For I have experienced much joy and encouragement from your love, because the hearts of the holy ones have been refreshed by you, brother."

As we build up and encourage those believers around us, we are filled with the Holy Spirit and the joy of the Lord. This fulfills our purpose as Christians.

Lord, while on earth, you showed us the way to live with our brothers and sisters. Give us the grace Lord to love them as you love them.

_____

_____

_____

_____

_____

_____

Psalm 94:19 "When cares increase within me, your comfort gives me your joy.''

God will always fill us with joy when we believe and trust Him. Trusting in Jesus, strengthens us and lead us into a deeper relationship with him.

Lord, increase our faith so that each moment of each day we may live in your joy.

_____
_____
_____
_____
_____
_____
_____
_____
_____

Isaiah 9:2 "You have brought them abundant joy and great rejoicing..."

God will always give us joy when we focus on how much he loves us. Pray and meditate on this reality each day.

Thank you, Lord, for your great and unconditional love for us! We love you with all our heart.

_____

_____

_____

_____

_____

_____

_____

_____

_____

_____

Psalm 98:4 "Shout with joy to the LORD, all the earth; break into song; sing praise."

When we praise the Lord with our voices and song, we are filled with his presence and joy. God inhabits the praises of his people!

Lord, help us to praise your name with great joy. May we sing and praise your name daily so that we are filled with our glory, grace, and joy.

_____

_____

_____

_____

_____

_____

_____

_____

Psalm 5:12 "Then all who trust in you will be glad and forever shout for joy.

You will protect them and those will rejoice in you who love your name." When we trust in the Lord, we are filled with His grace and joy. Trust leads to peace, then to greater love and joy.

Thank you, Lord, for your gift of peace. May we always trust in you, no matter the circumstance.

_____

_____

_____

_____

_____

_____

_____

_____

Psalm 66:2 "Shout joyfully to God, all the earth; sing of his glorious name; give him glorious praise."

We must not hide our joy under a bushel basket, but let everyone see how much we love the Lord.

Help us, Lord, sing your praises and shout for joy whether it is convenient or inconvenient.

_____

_____

_____

_____

_____

_____

_____

_____

_____

Isaiah 12:3 "With joy you will draw water from the foundations of salvation."

Jesus is the living water. In Him we will never thirst and will always have joy in our hearts.

Thank You, Lord, for being our living water and filling us with shouts of joy, leading us to Your great peace.

_____

_____

_____

_____

_____

_____

_____

_____

_____

_____

Sirach 1:12 "The fear of the Lord rejoices the heart, giving gladness, joy, and long life."

When we understand that God is all-sovereign, all-powerful, and all-loving, we are filled with his joy forever.

Lord, help us to understand how to reverently fear you, while understanding how much you love us. Fill our hearts with joy.

_____

_____

_____

_____

_____

_____

_____

_____

Luke 24:52 "They did him homage and then returned to Jerusalem with great joy."

Praise and worship, being in His presence and receiving the fruit of the spirit joy are all closely connected—intertwined spiritual experiences.

Lord, may our focus always be on you. Increase our joy when we worship your Holy name.

_____

_____

_____

_____

_____

_____

_____

_____

_____

Psalm 35:27 "But let those who favor my just cause shout for joy and be glad.

"May they ever say, 'Exalted be the LORD who delights in the peace of his loyal servant.'"

When we seek the Lord with all our heart, soul, might and strength, we are always filled with joy.

Lord, may we always seek your face and Your will. In so doing, we will be filled with Your grace, love and joy.

_____

_____

_____

_____

_____

PEACE

Clearly, peace is a fruit of the Holy Spirit that everyone strives to have in their hearts. What prevents that innermost state of peace? The world, sin, our own selfish desires and the absence of Jesus in our lives. Throughout His ministry, Jesus was unambiguous: He is the only way we truly can enjoy a peace that passes all understanding and lasts forever.

God did not leave us orphans, but has given us the Holy Spirit to guide us to Jesus and eternal peace. We become confused in our search for peace because we do not search for the source of all peace—Jesus. We must seek Jesus with all our heart, soul, mind and strength, and only then can we obtain the peace God so much wants to give us.

Philippians 4:6-7 "Have no anxiety at all, but in everything by prayer and petition, with thanksgiving, make your requests known to God. Then the peace of God that surpasses all understanding will guard your hearts and minds in Christ Jesus."

Peace comes from faith. Faith leads to trust and trust leads to peace.

Lord, we pray that we find true peace as we give you thanks for all you have done for us.

_____
_____
_____
_____
_____
_____
_____

Philippians 4:8b-9 "If there is any excellence and if there is anything worthy of praise, think about these things. Keep on doing what you have learned and received and heard and seen in me. Then the God of peace will be with you."

We must win the battlefield of the mind. Do not focus on your problems but on Who is always the solution!

Lord, please give us the wisdom and guidance of your Holy Spirit so that we may seek you through all of life's challenges.

_____

_____

_____

_____

_____

Colossians 3:15 "And let the peace of Christ control your hearts, the peace into which you were also called in one body. And be thankful."

Make thankfulness the motto of each day. Inscribe gratitude on your hearts. We will be protected against evil and dark thoughts!

Lord, we pray for a heart truly humble and thankful for your protection. Only you bring us peace

_____

_____

_____

_____

_____

_____

_____

1 Corinthians 7:15 "God has called you to peace."

Our Father's desire is that we have peace in our hearts each day and for eternity. Dismiss anxiety, repent and surrender your heart to Jesus!

May we come to know your eternal love, which can bring us only peace.

_____

_____

_____

_____

_____

_____

_____

_____

_____

James 3:18 "And the fruit of righteousness is its own in peace for those who cultivate peace."

Righteousness is being in "right relationship with God, doing the Father's will. True peace is possible only when we are doing God's will and are in His presence!

Lord, at times, we don't see your will as being our priority. You are our strength. We pray for your will so that we may truly have peace in our lives.

_____

_____

_____

_____

_____

_____

Romans 8:6 "The concern of the flesh is death, but the concern of the spirit is life and peace."

When the Holy Spirit takes over our lives, we feel a tremendous burst of love and peace!

Lord, we pray that we find the way to live fully in your Spirit. Give us the guidance to follow your will.

_____

_____

_____

_____

_____

_____

_____

_____

_____

Numbers 6:24-27 "The LORD bless you and keep you! The LORD let his face shine upon you! The LORD look upon you kindly, and give you peace!"

Let us pray this Scripture daily, and we will have peace that passes all understanding! This will allow us to remain in the presence of God.

We pray we can fully receive the peace You have in store for us, Lord. Help us to surrender and fully receive you in our hearts.

_____

_____

_____

_____

_____

_____

Isaiah 9:6a "His dominion is vast and forever peaceful."

God is the God of peace. Call upon his peace to fill your hearts and soul. He wants us to live in his peace always.

Lord, we pray for the humility to ask for Your peace. Bring us to our knees so that we may live in you.

_____

_____

_____

_____

_____

_____

_____

_____

_____

_____

PEACE

Galatians 5:22 "In contrast, the fruit of the Spirit is love, joy, peace, patience, kindness, generosity, faithfulness, gentleness, and self -control."

Call upon the Holy Spirit to give you the fruit of peace each and every day!

Lord, we pray that we may have eyes only for you. May we receive the peace that will guide us throughout our lives with your Holy Spirit.

_____

_____

_____

_____

_____

_____

_____

_____

Matthew 5:9 "Blessed are the peacemakers, for they will be called children of God."

Peace helps unify the Body of Christ by sharing love. The fruit of his love is Peace. When we are peacemakers, we are in the presence of God, doing His will!

Lord, we pray that we may be an instrument of peace for your children. May we receive your peace through the love of Jesus.

_____

_____

_____

_____

_____

_____

_____

Matthew 11:28 "Come to me, all you who labor and are burdened, and I will give you rest."

When we surrender our hearts to Jesus, resting in Him, we are filled with the Holy Spirit, which leads to love, peace and joy!

Lord, we ask for your Holy Spirit to rule our life so that we may rest in you and truly have peace.

_____

_____

_____

_____

_____

_____

_____

_____

_____

John 14:27 "Peace I leave with you; my peace I give to you. Not as the world gives do I give it to you. Do not let your hearts be troubled or afraid."

When we live in the "world" and not the spirit of God we find ourselves isolated and living in despair. When we have Jesus in our hearts and minds, when we surrender to him, we have peace that passes all understanding!

Lord, this world does its best to distract us from a life in you. Grant us the discernment to follow you in our daily life.

_____

_____

_____

_____

_____

John 16:33 "I have told you this so that you may have peace in me. In the world you will have trouble, but take courage, I have conquered the world."

Jesus is our Savior and conquered all evil when he died for our sins. Only in Jesus do we find peace. Do not expect anything of this world to give us true peace of mind, heart and soul.

Lord, help us believe that you are our future. Give us the courage to have a complete trust in you so that we may have peace and serve you totally.

_____

_____

_____

_____

_____

John 20:19 "Jesus came and stood in their midst and said, 'Peace be with you.'"

Each day Jesus stands with us, instructing us to keep our focus on him so that we may have everlasting peace!

Help us to recognize you in our lives Lord. Let us be sensitive to your gentle whisper. May we receive your gentle love and peace.

_____

_____

_____

_____

_____

_____

_____

_____

_____

PATIENCE

Patience is one fruit of the Holy Spirit that most of us struggle to achieve. Often, we see clearly when others lack patience, pointing it out to them or believing ourselves superior in this area. The reality is that we are in the biggest room in the world—the room for improvement.

In what circumstances do we lack patience? When we want something done in our time and in our way. In other words, we play "god" and think our way or timing is best. The personal quest for the gift of patience should cause us to repent of selfishness and the belief we know better than God what is best for us. It is critical that we trust in God's timing and in His way for us. Then this fruit will be attainable.

Numbers 14:18 "The LORD is slow to anger and abounding in kindness..."

Love conquers all. When we feel impatient, remember God's infinite patience with us! Ask the Lord to give you the gift of patience. This will lead to greater joy and kindness.

Holy Spirit, lead us through each day with the ability to love with your love and be patient with those around us. May we better understand your love for us and be thankful for the patience you have shown us.

_____
_____
_____
_____
_____

2 Peter 3:9 "The Lord...is patient with you, not wishing that any should perish but that all should come to repentance."

Even if we have committed the same sin 1,000 times, the Lord patiently waits for us to repent and come to Him completely.

Lord, we thank you for being patient with us and our sinful ways. We are humbled by your love for us.

_____

_____

_____

_____

_____

_____

_____

_____

_____

2 Corinthians 12:12 "The signs of an apostle were performed among you with endurance, signs and wonders, and mighty deeds."

When we are patient, we both allow and empower the Holy Spirit in our lives to perform great miracles! Expect and experience miracles in your life.

Lord, each day I wait for your plan to unfold before me. I am encouraged to know you are near and believe your plans for me are perfect. Help me to wait with expectative faith.

_____

_____

_____

_____

_____

_____

Galatians 5:22-23 "But the fruit of the Spirit is love, joy, peace, patience, kindness, generosity, faithfulness, gentleness, self-control. Against such there is no law."

Patience is a key fruit of the Holy Spirit. Love, joy, and peace are the catalysts for attaining more patience. God enhances holiness through the fruit of patience!

Please guide us, Lord, so that we can receive the fruit of patience. Teach us your ways so that we may glorify you in all that we do.

_____

_____

_____

_____

_____

Ephesians 4:1-3 "I, then, a prisoner for the Lord, urge you to live in a manner worthy of the call you have received, with all humility and gentleness, with patience, bearing with one another through love, striving to preserve the unity of the spirit through the bond of peace"

We must allow the love of Christ to be at the center of all our relationships. To experience the fruit of patience, we must ask for it and expect to receive it.

Help us to become ambassadors of peace. May your patience be in us.

_____

_____

_____

_____

_____

Colossians 1:11-12"...strengthened with every power, in accord with his glorious joy giving thanks to the Father, who has made you fit to share in the inheritance of the holy ones in light."

Jesus will give you His power to overcome trials, temptations and challenges. With the Holy Spirit, you will receive the patience you need to do the will of the Father.

Lord, give us the patience to endure through all life's challenges.

_____

_____

_____

_____

_____

_____

Colossians 3:12-13 "Put on then, as God's chosen ones, holy and beloved, heartfelt compassion, kindness, humility, gentleness, and patience, bearing with one another and forgiving one another, if one has a grievance against another; as the Lord has forgiven you, so must you also do."

As a disciple of Christ, we are to reflect his love, joy and patience with others, no matter how we are treated.

Lord, we ask for the grace that we may be patient.

_____

_____

_____

_____

_____

Luke 8:15 "...But as for the seed that fell on rich soil, they are the ones who, when they have heard the word, embrace it with a generous and good heart, and bear fruit through perseverance."

We must let the Word of God enter our hearts by reading, memorizing and praying Scripture. In response, our patience will increase

Thank you, Lord, for your Holy Scriptures. Grant us the patience to hear your words, live the Gospel and share it with your children.

_____

_____

_____

_____

_____

Romans 2:6-7 "…who will repay everyone according to his works: eternal life to those who seek glory, honor, and immortality through perseverance in good works..."

We must be patient with ourselves. as we strive for holiness. The Lord is shaping and molding us in His image and with His love.

Lord, we pray that we may be steadfast in following your ways. May we have patience to do your will in all things.

_____

_____

_____

_____

_____

_____

_____

_____

Romans 2:24-25 "For, as it is written, 'Because of you the name of God is reviled among the Gentiles.' Circumcision, to be sure, has value if you observe the law; but if you break the law, your circumcision has become uncircumcision."

Faith comes from perseverance through love and patience. We hope, knowing God is patient with us and will call us home at the appointed time.

Lord, at times life seems unbearable. May we be patient like you!

_____

_____

_____

_____

_____

_____

1 Timothy 1:16 "But for that reason I was mercifully treated, so that in me, as the foremost, Christ Jesus might display all his patience as an example for those who would come to believe in him for everlasting life."

When we trust in the Lord, we receive His patience and the peace that passes all understanding. We need endurance to do the will of the Lord!

Lord, may we trust in you during difficult times and have the endurance needed.

_____

_____

_____

_____

_____

_____

Hebrews 6:11-12 "We earnestly desire each of you to demonstrate the same eagerness for the fulfillment of hope until the end, so that you may not become sluggish, but imitators of those who, through faith and patience, are inheriting the promises."

Life is a test of endurance. The more we want things to happen, greater the need for patience. Sometimes God wants us to grow in our anticipation of his plan.

Even when we feel like quitting or giving up, we thank you Lord for not giving up on us.

_____

_____

_____

_____

_____

Romans 12:12 "Rejoice in hope, endure in affliction, persevere in prayer."

When we are tested through life's challenges and issues, we need to pray for patience. We most often want things to be fixed immediately, but God's timing is perfect!

Teach us, Lord, to have patience in every circumstance you place in our lives. Increase in us faith so that we may have hope in our future.

_____

_____

_____

_____

_____

_____

_____

Galatians 6:9 "Let us not grow tired of doing good, for in due time we shall reap our harvest, if we do not give up."

Patience leads to more faith and hope, which opens the door for more grace from the Lord. We must learn to live moment to moment with child-like faith.

Teach us, Lord, to never become discouraged in the midst of our challenges. Thank you for the gift of patience.

_____

_____

_____

_____

_____

_____

_____

Psalm 37:7 "Be still before the LORD; wait for him. Do not be provoked by the prosperous, nor by malicious schemers..."

When we are silent before the Lord, praying and listening, we are led with guidance to the fruit of the Spirit—greater patience.

Lord, help us in our prayer life to be still and know that you are always with us. May we hear your gentle reassurance.

_____

_____

_____

_____

_____

_____

_____

_____

Ephesians 4:2 "With all humility and gentleness, with patience, bearing with one another through love."

The greater the patience, the more likely our love for the Lord and each other will grow! May we carry our cross of humility with you guiding and helping us always.

Help us Lord with the gift of patience so that our love for others may grow and deepen each day. May we seek to glorify you Lord as we follow your footsteps.

_____

_____

_____

_____

_____

_____

_____

1 Corinthians 13:4 "Love is patient, love is kind. It is not jealous, [love] is not pompous, it is not inflated..."

When we love deeply, we are patient with the Lord and one another. We do not get angry, but let the gentleness of the Lord fill our hearts.

We cannot follow you without surrendering to your will. Help us, be patient with those to whom we are closest, especially our families.

_____

_____

_____

_____

_____

_____

_____

Romans 5:4 "And endurance, proven character, and proven character, hope."

When we endure life's challenges, we increase in holiness and grow closer to the Lord with our prayer life and the gifts of the Holy Spirit.

Teach us, Lord, how to grow in holiness through patience and always trusting in you.

_____
_____
_____
_____
_____
_____
_____
_____

Hebrews 6:15 "And so, after patient waiting, he obtained the promise."

When we are patient, God's promises and grace become evident in our lives. Look for them!

Lord, may we always rejoice in the strength, endurance and patience you give us to overcome life's challenges.

_____

_____

_____

_____

_____

_____

_____

_____

_____

_____

Revelation 2:19 "I know your works, your love, faith, service, and endurance, and that your last works are greater than the first."

Patience leads to faithfulness and doing the Lord's will in all our works and activities.   The greater the patience, the greater the faith and then greater the miracles.

Thank you Lord for teaching us how to do your will in all of our activities.

_____

_____

_____

_____

_____

_____

_____

Genesis 29:20 "So Jacob served seven years to get Rachel, but they seemed like only a few days to him because of his love for her."

When we are patient, God grants us the patience to endure suffering, ensuring that we reach our goal.

Holy Spirit, we ask that you give us the grace to endure the trials in our lives. Help us to surrender our very being and rely on you completely, so that we may have your patience to endure all trials in our lives.

_____

_____

_____

_____

_____

_____

_____

1 Samuel 13:8 "He waited seven days, until the appointed time Samuel had set, but Samuel did not come, and the army deserted Saul."

At times, we become impatient waiting on the Lord. No matter how long the Lord's answer takes, it is worth it!

Lord, we pray for a deeper trust in you and your Divine Will in our lives. May we grow patient as we wait with a joyful heart.

_____

_____

_____

_____

_____

_____

_____

_____

Luke 15:13 "After a few days, the younger son collected all his belongings and set off to a distant country where he squandered his inheritance on a life of dissipation."

"Lust" is defined as the impatient desire for something now, without delay. It never satisfies or fulfills us.

We ask you, Holy Spirit, to consume us with Love. We pray for the patience and increased faith to attain this relationship with you.

_____

_____

_____

_____

_____

_____

_____

Romans 8:25 "But if we hope for what we do not see, we wait with endurance."

When we have faith and trust in the Lord, we have the fruit of the Spirit, patience. It is important to ask for more patience in order to receive it.

Come Holy Spirit! Empty us of our doubt and lack of faith and fill us with the wisdom and grace to patiently await Your will.

_____
_____
_____
_____
_____
_____
_____
_____
_____

2 Thessalonians 1:4 "Accordingly, we ourselves boast of you in the churches of God regarding your endurance and faith in all your persecutions and the afflictions you endure."

When we are patient in our suffering, God will give us the grace and joy of the Lord! Ask the Lord for the grace of endurance when we have trials.

May we take comfort knowing the great love you have for us and feel Your consuming love as we live a life of joy.

_____

_____

_____

_____

_____

_____

Habakkuk 2:3 "For the vision is a witness for the appointed time, a testimony to the end; it will not disappoint. If it delays, wait for it, it will surely come, it will not be late."

We may need supernatural strength to have patience. Wait for it. God will grant your request!

Help us be patient as we strive to live in your Spirit and turn away from the life in the world.

_____

_____

_____

_____

_____

_____

_____

_____

Romans 5:3-4 "Not only that, but we even boast of our afflictions, knowing that affliction produces endurance, and endurance, proven character, and proven character, hope…"

Pray for the gift of perseverance. God will definitely provide it! Perseverance will lead to greater faith, gifts, and miracles.

Lord, deliver us from a life of misery by giving us counsel. Awaken in our soul a fiery love for you so that our heart burns for you alone.

_____

_____

_____

_____

_____

_____

Proverbs 14:29 "Long-suffering results in great wisdom; a short temper raises folly high."

When we endure our sufferings, and do not give in to anger, God will grant us the fruit of patience.

We pray for endurance through all trials to better serve you. Remind us Lord, we need your strength and patience to be the vessel of love you created us to be.

_____

_____

_____

_____

_____

_____

_____

Romans 12:12 "Rejoice in hope, endure in affliction, persevere in prayer."

Perseverance is the foundation of all patience. Ask for the Lord to grant it to you!

Lord, we ask that you remind us to pray for patience and to persevere as we face trials in our lives May we always see your hand in all that we are called to endure. May we increase in our faith to grow closer to you and abide in your loving arms.

_____

_____

_____

_____

_____

_____

_____

_____

Galatians 6:9 "Let us not grow tired of doing good, for in due time we shall reap our harvest, if we do not give up."

When we feel like giving up on our journey to God, we are close to the final victory. Do not give up!

Holy Spirit, we call on your help. May we see you as our solution, our comfort and joy. Grant us the patience to be faithful to You as we endure our difficulties and rely on you for our salvation and hope.

_____

_____

_____

_____

_____

_____

_____

Proverbs 16:32 "The patient are better than warriors, and those who rule their temper, better than the conqueror of a city."

When we are in battle with the enemy, patience is a tremendous weapon! Often, it is what we need to ensure victory against evil.

Lord, we ask for all your heavenly blessings and graces to be patient. May we wait for your command and seek your will.

_____

_____

_____

_____

_____

_____

Psalm 27:14 "Wait for the LORD, take courage; be stouthearted, wait for the LORD."

Courage from the Lord leads to patience, peace and joy! Ask the Lord for the gift of courage.

Strengthen our souls, Lord, so that we may completely trust in your ways. Give us the wisdom and strength of your Holy Spirit so that we are courageous in doing your will.

_____

_____

_____

_____

_____

_____

_____

Hebrews 10:36 "You need endurance to do the will of God and receive what he has promised."

God will test our endurance. When we turn to him and his timing, we will never regret it!

Lord, we surrender our lives to you. Renew our hearts, take over our lives and renew us with the power of your Holy Spirit. May our hearts long for you with great anticipation!

_____

_____

_____

_____

_____

_____

_____

Kindness

Kindness is an encouraging word or action, letting the love of Jesus flow through us.

When we put the other person's needs before ours, perhaps going out of our way to help meet the other's needs, we act with the mind and heart of Jesus.

To be kind is to have a cheerful attitude. To have a smile on our faces and a desire to care for others. A true act of kindness is sharing the Good News of Jesus Christ. In so many ways, the greatest kindness we can give someone is to share the certainty of God's ever-present, each one of us. Not to compromise but to love them enough to tell them the truth that Jesus is the way, the truth and the life.

Ephesians 4:32 "Be kind to one another, compassionate, forgiving one another as God has forgiven you in Christ."

When we are kind, we forgive; when the hurt is especially grievous, we can rely on God's grace to help us forgive. We do not answer evil with evil.

Help us, Lord, be compassionate in all that we say and do, so that everyone can see our kindness and love.

_____

_____

_____

_____

_____

_____

_____

_____

Hebrews 6:10 "For God is not unjust so as to overlook your work and the love you have demonstrated for his name by having served and continuing to serve the holy ones."

No one can outdo God's kindness and grace. Even if we don't truly deserve it, God showers us with blessings!

Lord, help us serve your people in all that we do. Help us to put you first and show your kindness in all we do.

_____

_____

_____

_____

_____

_____

_____

Romans 2:4 "Do you hold his priceless kindness, forbearance, and patience in low esteem, unaware that the kindness of God would lead you to repentance?"

It is critical that we take, open-hearted, God's marvelous gifts of repentance and the sacrament of reconciliation!

May we receive your kindness, Lord, by going to reconciliation often.

_____

_____

_____

_____

_____

_____

_____

_____

_____

Luke 6:35 "But rather, love your enemies and do good to them, and lend expecting nothing back; then your reward will be great and you will be children of the Most High, for he himself is kind to the ungrateful and the wicked."

Give to others without expecting anything in return and your reward in heaven will be great!

Help us, Lord, to love and be kind to those who hurt us with their words and actions. May we receive the grace to forgive them and return to them kind acts of love and compassion.

_____

_____

_____

_____

Colossians 3:12 "Put on then as God's chosen ones, holy and beloved, heartfelt compassion, kindness, humility, gentleness, and patience."

When we are kind, we are compassionate to others. Filled with the love of Christ, we embrace our heritage as God's "chosen ones."

We rejoice in your kindness Lord! Help us serve your people with a kind heart.

_____

_____

_____

_____

_____

_____

_____

_____

Proverbs 3:3 "Do not let love and fidelity forsake you; bind them around your neck; write them on the tablet of your heart."

Some translations have "kindness" instead of "fidelity." Never reject love and kindness; inscribe on our hearts. When we show love and fidelity, we demonstrate kindness.

We thank you, Lord, for your fidelity to us in spite of our weakness and sinfulness.

_____

_____

_____

_____

_____

_____

_____

_____

John 3:16 "For God so loved the world that he gave his only Son, so that everyone who believes in him might not perish but have eternal life."

The greatest "kindness" of all is Jesus' willing acceptance of death on a cross, which led to his resurrection and the gift to us of eternal salvation!

We do not deserve your kindness and forgiveness. Thank you Lord for your unconditional love.

_____

_____

_____

_____

_____

_____

_____

Micah 6:8 "You have been told, O mortal, what is good and what the Lord requires of you; Only to do justice and to love goodness, and to walk humbly with your God."

God's requests of us are so simple: only to be kind and merciful as he is kind and merciful.

Help us, Lord, to see your people through your eyes, so that we can be merciful as you are merciful to us.

_____

_____

_____

_____

_____

_____

_____

Romans 8:28 "We know that all things work for good for those who love God, who are called according to his purpose."

This is the foundation of the Lord's kindness: God turns whatever happens into good when we love and follow in His will.

Lord, thank you for your eternal kindness of turning our lives into good.

_____

_____

_____

_____

_____

_____

_____

_____

_____

Hebrews 13:2 "Do not neglect hospitality, for through it some have unknowingly entertained angels."

The gift of hospitality—welcoming and caring for the stranger—is extremely important in demonstrating the love of the Father.

Lord, teach us how to ask our guardian angel to pray for us and to be kind to all the people we see each day of our lives.

_____

_____

_____

_____

_____

_____

_____

Romans 12:10 "Love one another with mutual affection; anticipate one another in showing honor."

When we love each other intensely in the love of Jesus, we share his kindness in all that we do.

Lord, help us to passionately love your people and show them your love through kindness.

_____

_____

_____

_____

_____

_____

_____

_____

_____

Acts 28:2 "The natives showed us extraordinary hospitality; they lit a fire and welcomed all of us because it had begun to rain and was cold."

In our hour of need, those who are kind to us receive tremendous blessings and grace from the Lord.

Be our light, Lord, and help us show your love and hospitality always.

_____

_____

_____

_____

_____

_____

_____

_____

GENEROSITY

When giving a talk that includes asking for donations, I often joke that we politely mention to the Lord, "We don't want to be selfish, so You can keep the fruit of generosity." Generosity is what we want other people to show us.

Similar to all the fruit of the Holy Spirit, we must pray fervently—and sincerely desire—to embrace this fruit in our lives. We can't fake generosity. The sweet irony is when we give without compromise or expect nothing in return, God rewards us one hundredfold.

Acts 20:35 "...keep in mind the words of the Lord Jesus who himself said, 'It is more blessed to give than to receive.'"

When we approach each day with an openness in giving our time, talent, and treasure, we can be assured we will have a great day!

Thank you, Lord, for teaching us that no one can outdo your generosity. Help us to be generous with your love.

_____

_____

_____

_____

_____

_____

_____

_____

Luke 6:38 "Give and gifts will be given to you; a good measure, packed together, shaken down, and overflowing, will be poured into your lap. For the measure in which you measure will in return be measured out to you."

No one can out do God and His generosity. Everything we give with our heart will be returned to us a hundredfold!

Holy Spirit, teach us to love as you love your people.

_____

_____

_____

_____

_____

_____

_____

Proverbs 11:24 "One person is lavish and yet grows still richer; another is too sparing, yet is the poorer."

When we give from our heart, without expecting anything in return, God rewards us beyond our comprehension!

Lord, we pray that our generosity not be contingent on what we want out of a situation. May we be selfless in our generosity.

_____

_____

_____

_____

_____

_____

_____

_____

Proverbs 11:25 "Whoever confers benefits will be amply enriched, and whoever refreshes others will be refreshed."

When our focus is helping others with our gifts, we are lavished with even more blessings!

Lord, help us find those who are in need of our time, talent and treasure.

_____

_____

_____

_____

_____

_____

_____

_____

_____

_____

Luke 21:3-4 "...'I tell you truly, this poor widow put in more than all the rest; for those others have all made offerings from surplus wealth, but she, from her poverty, has offered her whole livelihood.'"

God knows when we are giving truly from our heart rather than what is simply convenient to our budget.

May we receive the gift of generosity and rejoice in using this gift routinely.

_____

_____

_____

_____

_____

_____

_____

_____

Matthew 6:21 "For where your treasure is, there also will your heart be."

God knows the desires of our hearts. Do we aspire to serve Jesus and His people? We will be paid accordingly.

Remind us, Lord, that we must seek your treasure and not the treasure of this world.

_____

_____

_____

_____

_____

_____

_____

_____

_____

_____

_____

1 Timothy 6:18 "Tell them to do good, to be rich in good works, to be generous, ready to share."

Everything we are given is for a purpose: to be used in service to God and his people. This includes our time, talent and treasure.

Lord, help us to be generous with the gifts you have given us.

_____

_____

_____

_____

_____

_____

_____

_____

_____

1 John 3:17 "If someone who has worldly means sees a brother in need and refuses him compassion, how can the love of God remain in him?"

Our love grows dramatically when we are generous and give from our hearts until it hurts!

Lord, give us the grace and listen to your Holy Spirit, so that we may become generous no matter the cost.

_____

_____

_____

_____

_____

_____

_____

_____

2 Corinthians 9:6 "Consider this: whoever sows sparingly, will also reap sparingly and whoever sows bountifully will also reap bountifully."

There are certain absolutes in life; this is one of them. When we give bountifully, we will be given infinite blessings!

Help us, Lord, to sow our gifts, talents and resources for you and your kingdom.

_____

_____

_____

_____

_____

_____

_____

_____

_____

Matthew 10:42 "And whoever gives only a cup of cold water to one of these little ones to drink because he is a disciple—amen, I say to you, he will surely not lose his reward."

When we are generous even in little things, our acts will be blessed and rewarded!

Help us, Lord, to open our eyes to everyone around us so that we may be the embodiment of your love.

_____

_____

_____

_____

_____

_____

_____

_____

2 Corinthians 9:7 "Each must do as already determined, without sadness or compulsion, for God loves a cheerful giver."

It is vital that we give not out of guilt, but out of love. When we love deeply—and with a smile—we give deeply.

Increase our love, Lord, for you and your people so that we may be generous in all that we say and do.

_____

_____

_____

_____

_____

_____

_____

_____

Matthew 6:3 "But when you give alms, do not let your left hand know what your right is doing."

Do not advertise your generosity. God sees what you do and will repay you accordingly with his riches and glory!

Thank you, Lord, for your generosity, for all the gifts and fruit of the Spirit you give us.

_____

_____

_____

_____

_____

_____

_____

_____

_____

_____

Acts 2:45 "They would sell their property and possessions and divide them among themselves all according to each one's need."

Let us give what we have to those who have not. We will never regret it!

Help us Lord, with never hold back in sharing of our time, talent and treasure with those in need.

_____

_____

_____

_____

_____

_____

_____

_____

_____

Matthew 25:35 "For I was hungry and you gave me food, I was thirsty and you gave me drink, a stranger and you welcomed me."

When we respond to those in need around us, those who are hungry for love and basic needs, our cup overflows with the grace of God for we are serving him.

Open our eyes, Lord, so as to see those who are in need of our love and resources.

_____

_____

_____

_____

_____

_____

_____

_____

Psalm 112:5 "It is good for the man gracious in lending, who conducts his affairs with justice."

When we lend money and don't necessarily expect to be repaid, our treasure in heaven will grow beyond measure!

Help us, Lord, be generous and give freely to all those in need. May the ability to give be enough for us.

_____

_____

_____

_____

_____

_____

_____

_____

Matthew 25:21 "His master said to him, 'Well done, my good and faithful servant. Since you were faithful in small matters, I will give you great responsibilities. Come, share your master's joy.'"

No act of love or generosity is wasted in the eyes of the Lord. Rejoice and be thankful!

Lord, help us to be faithful in every situation and circumstance no matter how big or small.

_____

_____

_____

_____

_____

_____

_____

Psalms 37:26 "All day long he is gracious and lends, and his offspring become a blessing."

When we are generous, we are blessed with our family and in our comings and goings.

Thank you, Lord, for helping us be generous and showering our families and loved ones with Your grace.

_____
_____
_____
_____
_____
_____
_____
_____
_____

Galatians 6:2 "Bear one another's burdens, and so you will fulfill the law of Christ."

When we put other people's needs first and help them with their challenges, we truly are living in the love of Christ!

Lord, we pray that we take great joy in serving you by helping others in life's challenges.

_____
_____
_____
_____
_____
_____
_____
_____

2 Corinthians 9:11 "You are being enriched in every way for all generosity, which through us produces thanksgiving to God."

God is so loving and generous to us. When we give of our hearts, the Lord smiles and blesses!

Lord, we pray that we may be generous with our love for you. May our heart rest in your Sacred Heart.

_____

_____

_____

_____

_____

_____

_____

_____

Hebrews 13:2 "Do not neglect hospitality, for through it some have unknowingly entertained angels."

When we are kind, when we are generous, we are surrounded by angels and filled with the love of Christ!

Lord, we pray that we are always generous and merciful, out of pure love for you.

_____

_____

_____

_____

_____

_____

_____

_____

_____

_____

FAITHFULNESS

To be faithful is to be filled with the Holy Spirit and the love of Jesus. We are told in Scripture that faith is necessary to please God. It is a gift that must be sought with all our heart and soul. Faithfulness is not a transient gift, but one that lasts forever. We may falter at times in faith, but God always gives faith back to us when we ask with earnest hears. To be faithful is to trust in God totally.

This fruit is critical to receiving the other fruit of the Spirit. When we have faith, we believe in God's goodness for us. We trust things will work out, and we need not fear. When we have faith, we are filled with His grace, peace, love and joy. With sincere hearts, we seek after, ask for and anticipate that we receive it unconditionally.

2 Corinthians 5:7 "For we walk by faith, not by sight."

Often, we are tested on the question of faith. Do you believe in what appears to be real or that which is truly real: Jesus.

May your grace be poured out in abundance upon us so that we may truly have faith to get out of the boat and walk in faith toward you.

_____

_____

_____

_____

_____

_____

_____

_____

_____

FAITHFULNESS

Galatians 5:22-23 "In contrast, the fruit of the Spirit is love, joy, peace, patience, kindness, generosity, faithfulness, gentleness, self-control."

When we ask for more of the Holy Spirit, we will receive more of the fruit of the Spirit. Our faithfulness will grow dramatically!

Holy Spirit, we pray to you for all the grace you have for us. Increase our faith to believe in the blessings you have for us.

_____

_____

_____

_____

_____

_____

_____

John 14:15 "If you love me, you will keep my commandments."

The Lord asks us to be faithful in all our endeavors. Pray that your faith is strong enough!

Lord, your gift of faith is essential in living a Christian life. Please grant the grace of faith and increase it, as my heart is opened to you more each day.

_____

_____

_____

_____

_____

_____

_____

_____

_____

Luke 12:42 "And the Lord replied, 'Who, then, is the faithful and prudent servant whom the master will put in charge of his servants to distribute [the] food allowance at the proper time?'"

God has put each of us in charge of certain responsibilities. Are we faithful and obedient or do we procrastinate and not fulfill what God desires from us?

Lord, fill us with your Holy Spirit and set our hearts on fire, to serve you in all matters of our lives.

_____

_____

_____

_____

_____

_____

1 John 1:9 "If we acknowledge our sins, he is faithful and just and will forgive our sins and cleanse us from every wrongdoing."

Rejoice! God is merciful and just. He forgives us when we acknowledge him and ask forgiveness of our sins.

Lord, you are truly merciful when we sin. Help us to always come to you. We want to reunite with you as we turn to you with a contrite heart.

_____

_____

_____

_____

_____

_____

_____

_____

1 Corinthians 10:13 "No trial has come to you but what is human. God is faithful and will not let you be tried beyond your strength; but with the trial he will also provide a way out, so that you may be able to bear it."

Even when experiencing a major trial, when we can see no way out, we can trust in Jesus. He will give us the strength we need to overcome the challenge.

Lord, increase our faith so that we understand that you are with us every step we take.

_____

_____

_____

_____

_____

Psalm 91:4 "He will shelter you with his pinions, and under his wings you may take refuge; God's faithfulness is a protecting shield."

God is our shelter and our shield. We must always remember we are never alone. God is with us always!

We praise your name for protecting us against all evil and being our eternal shield.

_____

_____

_____

_____

_____

_____

_____

_____

_____

Proverbs 20:6 "Many say, 'My loyal friend,' but who can find someone worthy of trust?'

To be trustworthy is to be faithful to our Lord's commandments.

Lord, give us your strength and courage not to compromise in our love and obedience to you.

_____

_____

_____

_____

_____

_____

_____

_____

_____

_____

2 Timothy 2:13 "If we are unfaithful he remains faithful, for he cannot deny himself."

God is 100% faithful. We need never fear; God's love is unconditional and will never be withdrawn. It is there forever!

Thank you, Lord, for always being at our side and being true to your promises.

_____

_____

_____

_____

_____

_____

_____

_____

_____

_____

FAITHFULNESS

Proverbs 3:3 "Do not let love and fidelity forsake you; bind them around your neck; write them on the tablet of your heart."

When we are faithful, God is faithful to us with infinite blessings. Rejoice!

Lord, help us to run the race of being faithful to your word, your commandments and your love. We long to hear the words, "Well done my good and faithful servant."

_____

_____

_____

_____

_____

_____

_____

_____

_____

FAITHFULNESS

Revelation 2:10 "...Remain faithful until death, and I will give you the crown of life."

Seek faithfulness each day and in everything you do. You will be rewarded with the crown of life for all of eternity!

Lord, we seek the crown of life with all our heart and soul. Give us the grace to achieve this worthy goal.

_____

_____

_____

_____

_____

_____

_____

_____

_____

_____

FAITHFULNESS

Matthew 10:22 "You will be hated by all because of my name, but whoever endures to the end will be saved."

When we are faithful to the end—even in the face of the world's rejections—we receive blessings for all of eternity!

Lord, we ask for your help and grace for the gift of faith so that we may never waiver in our trials.

_____

_____

_____

_____

_____

_____

_____

_____

Hebrews 11:6 "But without faith it is impossible to please him, for anyone who approaches God must believe he exists and that he rewards those who seek him."

Faith moves mountains. When we are faithful to the Lord, He rewards us with greater faith. Rejoice!

We praise you for your great gift of faith— the only faith that will move the mountains in our lives.

_____

_____

_____

_____

_____

_____

_____

_____

FAITHFULNESS

Psalms 31:24 "Love the LORD, all you who are faithful to him. The LORD protects the loyal but repays the arrogant in full."

The greatest sign of faithfulness is the degree of love we have for the Lord. Love him with all your heart forever!

Help us, Lord, increase our love for you so that we never waiver in our faith.

_____

_____

_____

_____

_____

_____

_____

_____

_____

Exodus 34:6 "...The LORD, the LORD, a God gracious and merciful, slow to anger and abounding in love and fidelity."

No one can ever come close to God's faithfulness to him. Trust in Jesus!

Lord, thank you for your great mercy and love for us. We rejoice in our covenant with you!

_____

_____

_____

_____

_____

_____

_____

_____

_____

_____

Galatians 3:9 "Consequently, those who have faith are blessed along with Abraham who had faith."

Faith is the foundation of our love for God. Ask and seek more faith, and you will receive it, along with more love for God and His people!

Lord, we ask for an increase in our faith. We thank you for giving us an increase of faith.

_____

_____

_____

_____

_____

_____

_____

_____

1 Timothy 5:8 "And who ever does not provide for relatives and especially family members has denied the faith and is worse than a nonbeliever."

Our faithfulness requires us to take care of those closest to us. We must trust God will supply what we need, according to his richness and glory!

Lord, our desire is to faithfully serve your people. Help us stand up for you and your faithful teachings.

_____

_____

_____

_____

_____

_____

_____

Hebrews 3:5-6 "Moses was 'faithful in his house' as a 'servant' to testify to what would be spoken, but Christ was faithful as a son placed over his house."

How faithful are you to your family, friends, community and, most of all, the Lord?

Lord, help us to faithfully love your children.

_____

_____

_____

_____

_____

_____

_____

_____

_____

_____

Philippians 1:6 "I am confident of this, that the one that began a good work in you will continue to complete it until the day of Christ Jesus."

Do not be discouraged. Do not lose your confidence. Continue doing what God has called you to do. God remains with you always

Lord, may our eyes always be on you so that we may never lose confidence in ourselves or our future.

_____

_____

_____

_____

_____

_____

_____

Hosea 2:22 "I will betroth you to me with fidelity and you shall know the LORD."

God has called us as His adoptive children to know him, love him and serve him. Rejoice and be filled with his love and Holy Spirit!

We praise you, Lord, for being our Father. May we serve you always with all our heart.

_____

_____

_____

_____

_____

_____

_____

_____

_____

GENTLENESS

Gentleness is a fruit of the Spirit we don't think about routinely. In fact, at times we see it as a weakness. To some of us, gentleness is similar to meekness, implying a degree of dysfunction. We often desire to be strong, aggressive and forceful. We consider gentleness a quality of the weak. However, to be gentle, particularly in the face of anger or hatred, requires a strong heart and will

To be gentle is to embrace the love of Jesus in our hearts. We know Jesus does not "bruise a broken reed." He is gentle and treats us with a tender love that lasts forever.

Let us ask and strive for a gentle heart and always make gentleness the foundation of our thoughts and actions.

GENTLENESS

Galatians 5:22-23 "In contrast, the fruit of the Spirit is love, joy, peace, patience, kindness, generosity, faithfulness, gentleness, self-control."

Seek the fruit of the Spirit. Continue to strive for gentleness in all your comings and goings.

Lord, may everyone we are with daily see your gentleness and love in us.

_____
_____
_____
_____
_____
_____
_____
_____
_____

Ephesians 4:2 "With all humility and gentleness, with patience, bearing with one another through love."

To have a gentle spirit means to love intensely and be patient and forgiving with one another.

Help us to be gentle in spirit each day. May we serve you with a gentle spirit.

_____

_____

_____

_____

_____

_____

_____

_____

_____

_____

GENTLENESS

2 Corinthians 10:1 "Now I myself, Paul, urge you through the gentleness and clemency of Christ, I who am humble when face to face with you, but brave toward you when absent."

Scripture tells us that Christ is so gentle He will not bruise a broken reed. Let us do the same!

Lord, may our lives reflect your gentleness in all our relationships, especially with those closest to us.

_____

_____

_____

_____

_____

_____

_____

James 3:17 "But the wisdom from above is first of all pure, then peaceable, gentle, compliant, full of mercy and good fruits, without inconstancy or insincerity."

When we are full of the wisdom of Christ, we are filled with love, joy and the gentleness that comes from his presence.

To have a gentle spirit is to have the Spirit of the Lord.

_____

_____

_____

_____

_____

_____

_____

_____

_____

GENTLENESS

2 Timothy 2:24 "A slave of the Lord should not quarrel, but should be gentle with everyone, able to teach, tolerant."

When we are filled with the Holy Spirit, we take on the gentle spirit of Christ.

Teach us, Lord, to ask for the Holy Spirit to be released in our life so that we have a gentle spirit.

_____

_____

_____

_____

_____

_____

_____

_____

_____

_____

Matthew 11:29 "Take my yoke upon you and learn from me, for I am meek a humble of heart; and you will find rest for yourselves."

The gentleness of the Lord is where we find rest and joy!

Help us, Lord, to take on your yoke and find rest in you.

_____

_____

_____

_____

_____

_____

_____

_____

_____

_____

Colossians 3:12 "Put on then, as God's chosen ones, holy and beloved, heartfelt compassion, kindness, humility, gentleness, and patience." (repeated on pages 78 and 112)

As a lover of Christ and His people, we are to adopt all of these attributes. Gentleness leads to patience and kindness.

Help us, Lord, to be generous with your gentleness.

_____

_____

_____

_____

_____

_____

_____

_____

Galatians 6:1 "Brothers, even if a person is caught in some transgression, you who are spiritual should correct that one in a gentle spirit, looking to yourself, so that you also may not be tempted."

To be gentle means that you have the love and compassion of Christ for others. Not judging, but filled with the Holy Spirit!

Help us, Lord, not to be judgmental but to have a gentle spirit.

_____

_____

_____

_____

_____

_____

_____

_____

GENTLENESS

1 Peter 3:16 "But do it with gentleness and reverence, keeping your conscience clear, so that, when you are maligned, those who defame your good conduct in Christ may themselves be put to shame."

When you are in conflict with those who seek to harm you, the fruit of gentleness will help you treat them with gentleness.

Thank you, Lord, for giving us your fruit of gentleness with those who are not supporting us.

_____

_____

_____

_____

_____

_____

_____

1 Thessalonians 2:7 "Although we were able to impose our weight as apostles of Christ. Rather, we were gentle among you, as a nursing mother cares for her children."

As a mother gently loves her child, how much more does the Lord gently love us?

We praise you, Lord, for helping us be gentle with those in our life.

_____

_____

_____

_____

_____

_____

_____

_____

_____

SELF-CONTROL

God desires that we are disciplined in our walk with Him. We can't be on an emotional roller coaster. It is critical that we not be a slave to our emotions. To have self-control is to be indifferent to what the world brings to us. Circumstances don't matter. Only Jesus is important to us.

It is important we desire self-control in every part of our lives. Our thoughts, words and habits must center on Jesus.

To have self-control is to lead a life of self-examination. We must strive constantly to increase our self-control by first seeking Jesus with all our heart and surrendering our lives to Him. Like layers of an onion that are peeled one at a time, our increase in self-control is often gradual. Let's strive for it and know that our lives are a journey not a single event.

Proverbs 29:11 "Fools give vent to all their anger, but the wise, biding their time, control it."

Self-control is about letting Jesus in us be stronger than any anger we have toward other people.

Lord, despite our feelings of anger, we ask You to give us the grace to control our thoughts and words as we endure the challenges before us.

_____

_____

_____

_____

_____

_____

_____

_____

Galatians 5:22-23 "In contrast, the fruit of the Spirit is love, joy, peace, patience, kindness, generosity, faithfulness, gentleness, self-control. Against such there is no law."

If we allow the Holy Spirit fill us with love, joy, peace, patience and the other fruit, we will have self-control.

Lord, we pray for a great trust in you. May you bring us to a life of holiness, which will bring you glory.

_____

_____

_____

_____

_____

_____

_____

Titus 1:8 "[Be]...hospitable, a lover of goodness, temperate, just, holy, and self-controlled."

It is critical that we live a life distinguished by self-control, which leads to a life of holiness.

Lord, we desperately need your help. Create in us a heart united with you. May our self-control be a message of love for all.

_____

_____

_____

_____

_____

_____

_____

James 1:19 "Know this, my dear brothers: everyone should be quick to hear, slow to speak, slow to wrath."

TO listen to the Lord means we let God speak through us in measured ways.

Lord, we pray for the self-control to be your devoted child who awaits your gentle whisper. May we look to you for guidance on how to live in you.

_____

_____

_____

_____

_____

_____

_____

_____

_____

Proverbs 21:23 "Those who guard mouth and tongue guard themselves from trouble."

Are you a person who speaks first and thinks later? Let the Lord use your mind to think and speak appropriately.

Lord, we pray for your grace to consume our heart, so that we may bring you glory through words of love and show self-control. May we adhere to your will.

_____

_____

_____

_____

_____

_____

_____

_____

Isaiah 53:7 "Though harshly treated, he submitted and did not open his mouth; Like a lamb led to slaughter or a sheep silent before shearers, he did not open his mouth."

When we are harshly treated by someone, look to our Lord's example of not responding in kind.

Lord, we pray that we may stop to pray for Your love and compassion. Help us be a vessel of your mercy.

_____

_____

_____

_____

_____

_____

_____

Proverbs 18:7 "The mouths of fools are their ruin; their lips are a deadly snare."

Use your speech to build up and encourage, not to tear down or judge.

Lord, we pray for good judgement to share encouraging gestures of love toward all those with whom we come into contact. May we be a purified vessel of Your love and always act with great self-control.

_____

_____

_____

_____

_____

_____

_____

_____

_____

Proverbs 29:18 "Without a vision the people lose restraint; but happy is the one who follows instructions."

When we listen to the Lord and follow His desires, we have the joy of the Lord!

Lord, give us the grace to follow your will in our Life. May we surrender all of our heart and soul to you for your glory.

_____

_____

_____

_____

_____

_____

_____

_____

_____

Acts 24:25 "But as he spoke about righteousness and self-restraint and the coming judgement, Felix became frightened..."

When we have self-control, others find it challenging because they are not used to it. Let the Holy Spirit lead you!

Lord, we will trust in your wisdom and follow you by exemplifying the self-control you require of us. We will trust in you forever!

_____

_____

_____

_____

_____

_____

_____

1 Corinthians 7:9 "But if they cannot exercise self-control they should marry, for it is better to marry than to be on fire."

The Lord is very clear: we must exercise self-control with our bodies and sexuality.

Lord, may we have purity of thought. May we pray daily that your children turn to you in thought, word and deed and exercise self-control.

_____

_____

_____

_____

_____

_____

_____

_____

_____

Romans 6:12 "Therefore, sin must not reign over your mortal bodies so that you obey their desires."

Focus on purity of heart and soul so that you may see God!

Lord, you know all our thoughts and intentions. you know our weaknesses; purify our hearts so that we may be a worthy vessel of your love.

_____

_____

_____

_____

_____

_____

_____

_____

_____

Revelation 21:7 "The victor will inherit these gifts, and I shall be his God, and he will be my son."

We need to keep our eye on the prize. Obey God and we will be with him for eternity!

Lord, you are our future! Bring us to your Sacred Heart so that we may abide in your righteousness.

_____

_____

_____

_____

_____

_____

_____

_____

Job 31:1 "I made a covenant with my eyes not to gaze upon a virgin."

Control your thoughts and any possible lust by practicing self-control with your eyes.

Lord, purify our heart with the fire of your love. May we be pure and chaste and have eyes for only you.

_____

_____

_____

_____

_____

_____

_____

_____

_____

_____

Luke 6: 27 "But to you who hear I say, love your enemies, do good to those who hate you."

It is important to love everyone, especially those who hurt or abuse you, for to do so is following Christ's example!

Lord, you know our struggles when we are hurting. Give us the strength to be your meek children and love those who hurt us.

_____

_____

_____

_____

_____

_____

_____

_____

Made in the USA
Columbia, SC
10 June 2019